NATIONAL
GEOGRAPHIC
KiDS

GO WiLD!
Elephants

Margie Markarian

NATIONAL GEOGRAPHIC
WASHINGTON, D.C.

Sound the trumpets!

Elephants are the BIGGEST land animals in the world. They are also one of the strongest, smartest, and *NOSE-IEST!*

Let's learn all about elephants together.

Stomping Grounds

Elephants live in Africa and Asia. They live in many different types of habitats.

Most live on sunny grasslands.

STOMP! STOMP!

Some live in shady forests and jungles.

TROMP! TROMP!

Others spend their days in sandy deserts or muddy swamps.

CLOMP! CLOMP!

7

Home Turf

The weather where elephants live is usually warm or hot.

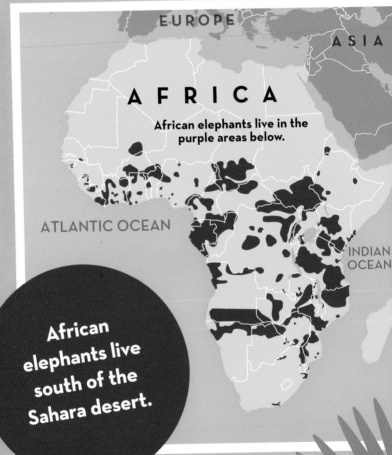

AFRICA

African elephants live in the purple areas below.

ATLANTIC OCEAN

EUROPE

ASIA

INDIAN OCEAN

African elephants live south of the Sahara desert.

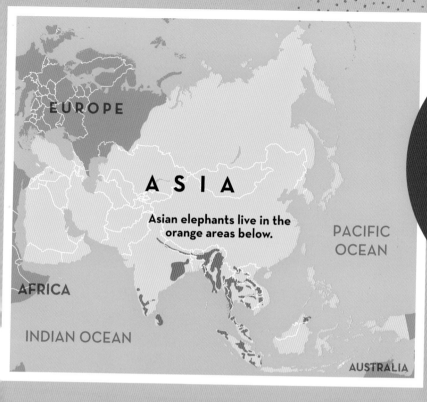

EUROPE

A S I A

Asian elephants live in the orange areas below.

PACIFIC OCEAN

AFRICA

INDIAN OCEAN

AUSTRALIA

Asian elephants are spread across South Asia and Southeast Asia, including some islands.

Living Large

Elephants are ENORMOUS.

From toe to shoulder, the tallest African elephants stand 13 feet (4 m) high. That's taller than a basketball hoop! They weigh as much as 14,000 pounds (6,350 kg). That's about as heavy as two pickup trucks.

Busy Bodies

Elephants have some amazing body parts.

TAIL: Wiry hairs on the end of an elephant's tail are great for swatting away flies.

SKIN: All that wrinkly skin helps elephants keep cool. The wrinkles hold water that falls from raindrops or that elephants spray.

LEGS: Long and massive legs support all that body weight.

FEET: Thickly padded feet help an elephant keep its balance.

EARS: Flappy, floppy ears help elephants keep cool, especially when they use them as fans.

TUSKS: Tusks are teeth that grow outside the body.

TRUNK: The tip of an elephant's trunk has fingerlike lobes for touching and picking things up.

Nosing Around!

An elephant's trunk is long and flexible. It helps an elephant breathe, smell, eat, and drink. But that's not all. Elephants also use them to ...

HUG and say HELLO,

PUSH and PULL,

SPRAY and SQUIRT,

TOOT and TRUMPET!

Cool Tool!

Tusks are sharp, hard, and made of ivory. They are teeth that never stop growing. The older the elephant, the LOOOOOOOONGER the tusks.

Elephants use their tusks to dig water holes, pull plants, lift objects, and protect themselves.

Tusks are a handy place to rest a weary trunk, too.

Celebrating Differences

All elephants are special, but these three types of Asian elephants are extra special. They have features that set them apart from other elephants.

Sri Lankan elephants are the darkest in color.

Borneo pygmy elephants are the smallest.

Sumatran elephants are the lightest in color.

All three of these kinds of elephants live on islands. Good thing elephants know how to SWIM and SNORKEL.

Going Green

Elephants are herbivores. That means they eat only plants and no meat.

They can even make a meal out of a tree! All it takes is ...

a STRETCH to grab some leaves,

a **SCRITCH-SCRATCH** to peel off bark,

and a **HEAVE-HO** to turn up tasty roots.

21

Long Walks to Water

A full-grown elephant drinks as much as 60 gallons (227 L) of water daily. That's about as much water as you use to fill your bathtub.

GULP! GULP!

At hot times of the year when there is little rain, some elephants walk long distances to find water. The oldest female leads the migration. She has the best memory and remembers where all the best watering holes are.

It looks like a game of follow the leader!

Grandmas Rule!

Elephants are social animals. They like being with other elephants. Family groups often travel together in herds. Females stay with their families all their lives. The oldest and wisest female is called the matriarch. She is in charge of the herd.

Male elephants leave their mothers when they are between 12 and 15 years old. They may join an all-male herd or live alone.

Group Hug, Group Huddle

Elephants have feelings.
They are sad when a
family member dies.
They are excited when
friends visit and new
babies are born.

WOO-HOO!

Listen Up!

Elephants use many sounds to communicate. Some of their RUMBLES are so low-pitched that humans can't hear them. But other elephants can hear them from miles away. Elephants also use their bodies to talk.

They stick out their ears to say "Stay away!"

They hug trunks to say "I like you!"

A tap from behind means "Time to GO, GO, GO!"

Big Babies

Compared to other mammals, newborn elephants are JUMBO. They weigh about 200 pounds (91 kg) and stand three feet (0.9 m) tall. That's about the size of a washing machine!

Young elephants are called calves. The whole herd helps a new mom protect and care for her calf.

1 year:
A calf weighs
about 1,000
pounds (454 kg).

At birth:
Newborns stand up
on day one and start
walking soon after.

2–10 years:
At two, it's bye to baby
teeth. Make way for
molars, then tusks.

12–15 years: Young males leave home, but young females stay with their herd.

18 years: Elephants reach adulthood but may keep growing in size until age 25.

70 years: Elephants in the wild can live to be 70 years old.

Since elephants eat only plants, their poop is full of seeds. The seeds they poop grow into new plants and help keep forests and grasslands green and healthy.

Sometimes young elephants play games using stones, plants, or sticks.

Even though they are big, elephants can walk at speeds up to 25 miles an hour (40 km/h). That's as fast as a car might drive through a neighborhood.

Baby elephants sometimes comfort themselves by sucking their trunks, just like baby humans suck their thumbs.

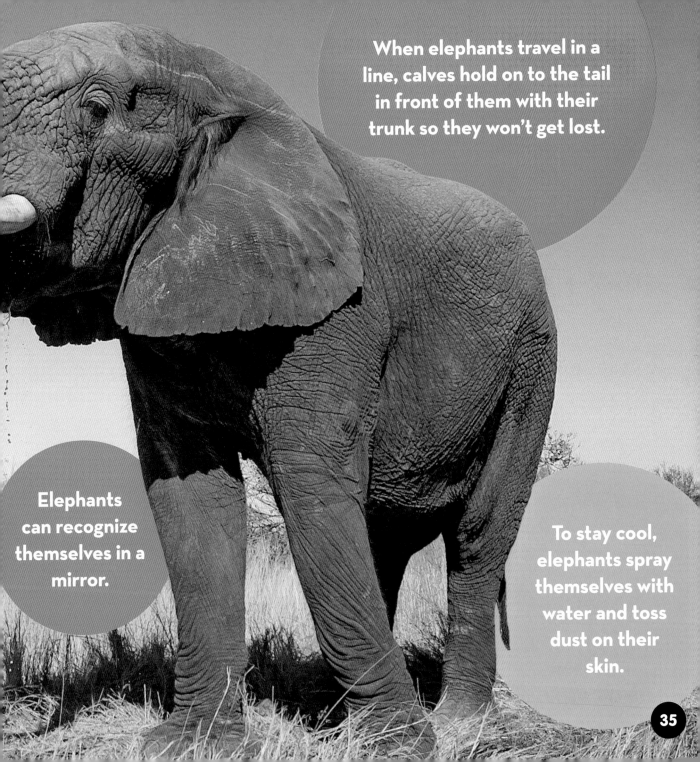

When elephants travel in a line, calves hold on to the tail in front of them with their trunk so they won't get lost.

Elephants can recognize themselves in a mirror.

To stay cool, elephants spray themselves with water and toss dust on their skin.

Elephant Troubles

Millions of elephants once roamed across Africa and Asia. Today, there are only about 465,000 elephants left in the wild.

Through the years, the number of elephants dropped because people hunted them for their valuable ivory tusks.

The elephant population also fell because people built farms, homes, and other buildings where elephants live.

Hunting and loss of land are still threats

Helping Elephants

Many people want to protect elephants.

People passed laws against hunting elephants and selling ivory. They created computer programs to help people find hunters before they can hurt elephants.

In Africa, they protected more land for elephants.

AT THE HOEDSPRUIT ENDANGERED SPECIES CENTRE IN SOUTH AFRICA, TWO GUARDS AND THEIR HIGHLY TRAINED DOG, ZEE, CHECK FOR HUNTERS.

In Asia, they designed special fences and pathways to prevent elephants and people from disturbing each other's spaces.

Aiding Elephants

You can help elephants, too.

Start by sharing what you know and love about elephants with friends. Talk to them about not buying jewelry, art, or other items made of ivory.

You can also celebrate World Elephant Day on August 12. That's when people all over the world sign a promise to protect elephants and their habitats.

Every promise counts!

Guess My Size

Elephants are the world's biggest land animals.

See if you can put these other animals in order from largest to smallest!

baboon

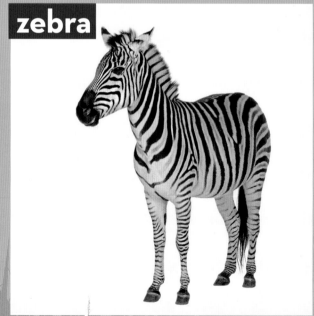

zebra

fox

hippopotamus

hedgehog

BONUS FUN:
Do you know what
animal is bigger
than an elephant?
Here's a hint:
It's a blue-gray color and
swims in the ocean.

Answers from largest to smallest: hippopotamus, zebra, baboon, fox, hedgehog. BONUS FUN answer: blue whale

Want to build your child's enthusiasm for elephants?

Kids will be amazed by an elephant's sheer size, that remarkable trunk, and everything a trunk can do! If you can't get to a zoo, watching videos online is the next best thing. You can check out awesome elephant videos and articles on the National Geographic Kids website at natgeokids.com.

Here are some other activities for you and your child to do together.

Spread Elephant Awareness
(Research, Write, and Draw)

Help your child research items that are traditionally made from ivory (jewelry, statues, art objects, decorative combs, chess pieces, very old piano keys). Then create a poster displaying some of these objects. Top it off with a drawing of an elephant and a headline that discourages the purchase of ivory items. Hang the poster in a place where visiting friends and relatives can see it. You can also encourage your child to take it to school to share with their teacher and classmates.

Elephant Concentration
(Public Speaking and Writing)

Invite your child to draw picture pairs of these six elephant body parts on index cards: trunk, tail, tusk, leg, eye, ear (for a total of 12 pictures). Shuffle the cards and place them facedown on a table or the floor. Take turns turning over two cards, trying to find the matches. The person with the most matches when the game is over gets to say, "I have a memory like an elephant."

 ## Enormous Elephant Reading Week
(Reading and Public Speaking)

Enhance your child's reading experience about real elephants with more books. Head to the library and take out up to seven books about elephants. They can be a mix of fiction and nonfiction. Read each day for a week, and at the end of the week, invite your child to "show and tell" about his or her favorite book or part of a book.

 ## Miles to Migrate
(Math and Map Skills)

Elephants sometimes walk 120 miles (193 km) a day as they search for food and water during a migration. To help your child understand how far that is, work together to locate your town on a map and then identify places 120 miles to the north, south, east, and west. Discuss how long you think it would take to get to those places by car, using public transportation, and on foot. Then use a maps app to see how close your guesses were.

 ## Adopt an Elephant
(Responsibility)

No, your family doesn't actually get to bring an elephant home, but adoption programs give you and your child a way to help an elephant have a safer and healthier life. The Sheldrick Wildlife Trust, the World Wildlife Fund, and the Elephant Listening Project have "adoption" programs based on different levels of giving.

calf: a baby elephant

communicate: to pass on information

habitat: an animal's natural home

herbivore: an animal that eats only plants

herd: two or more family groups of elephants

ivory: the yellowish white substance that forms elephant tusks

mammals: a group of animals, including humans, that have backbones, are warm-blooded, breathe air, have hair or fur, and drink milk from their mother

matriarch: the female leader of an elephant family group

migration: the movement from one region or habitat to another to find food or a mate

savanna: a large flat area of grassy land with very few trees

For Dad, who loved watching animal shows and sharing fun animal facts —M.M.

Cover, fishcat007/Adobe Stock; Back cover, Susan Schmitz/Shutterstock; 1, Andy Rouse/naturepl; 5, HeresTwoPhotography/Adobe Stock; 6, Kenneth Canning/Getty Images; 7 (UP), Thomas Jurkowski/Dreamstime; 7 (LO), Education Images/Getty Images; 8-9, NG Maps; 8, Thomas Retterath/Getty Images; 9, Yashpal Rathore/NPL/Minden Pictures; 10-11, Richard Carey/Adobe Stock; 12-13, Susan Schmitz/Shutterstock; 14, Anup Shah/naturepl; 15 (UP LE), Leon/Adobe Stock; 15 (UP RT), Thierry GRUN/Alamy Stock Photo; 15 (LO), Isabelle/Adobe Stock; 17, Manoj Shah/Getty Images; 18, David/Adobe Stock; 19 (LE), Biosphoto/Alamy Stock Photo; 19 (RT), Christian Loader/Scubazoo; 20, Jeryco/Getty Images; 21 (UP), blickwinkel/Alamy Stock Photo; 21 (LO), Lionela Rob/Alamy Stock Photo; 22, Villiers/Adobe Stock; 23, Sergey Novikov/Adobe Stock; 24, fishcat007/Adobe Stock; 25, John Warburton-Lee Photography/Alamy Stock Photo; 27, Michael Poliza; 28, Tony Heald/NPL/Minden Pictures; 29 (UP), Alta Oosthuizen/Adobe Stock; 29 (LO), Suzi Eszterhas/Minden Pictures; 31, Four Oaks/Shutterstock; 32 (LE), worradirek/Shutterstock; 32 (CTR), Michael Nichols, NGS; 32 (RT), Ferrero-Labat/Auscape Minden Pictures; 33 (LE), Jean-Francois Ducasse/Alamy Stock Photo; 33 (CTR), Karlos Lomsky/Adobe Stock Photo; 33 (RT), Martin Withers/FLPA/Minden Pictures; 34-35, Donovan van Staden/Shutterstock; 36, Martin Harvey/Getty Images; 37, Phototography by Mangiwau/Getty Images; 38, Ilan Godfrey/Getty Images; 39, Lakruwan Wanniarachchi/Getty Images; 40, Edmond So/Getty Images; 41, Pacific Press Media Production Corp./Alamy Stock Photo; 42 (LE), Eric Isselee/Shutterstock; 42 (RT), Eric Isselee/Shutterstock; 43 (UP LE), Eric Isselee/Shutterstock; 43 (UP RT), Eric Isselee/Shutterstock; 43 (LO), Dixi_/Adobe Stock

Published by National Geographic Partners, LLC, Washington, DC 20036.

Designed by Kathryn Robbins

Hardcover ISBN: 978-1-4263-7256-8
Reinforced library binding ISBN: 978-1-4263-7257-5

The author and publisher wish to acknowledge the expert review of this book by ecologist and elephant conservationist Dominique Gonçalves and the National Geographic book team: Angela Modany, associate editor; Shelby Lees, senior editor; Sarah J. Mock and Nicole DiMella, photo editors; Mike McNey, senior cartographer; Alix Inchausti, production editor; and Anne LeongSon and Gus Tello, design production assistants.

Printed in Hong Kong
21/PPHK/1